ONE WORLD
ONE CHILD

EXPRESSIONS OF CHILDHOOD

By DIANNA LYNN

PHOTOGRAPHS BY YOSHIAKI NAGASHIMA WITH LYRICS BY JOE HENRY

Additional images by Nicholas DeVore III, Paul Chesley, David Hiser, Chris Rainier and Melinda Berge

Published by ARC International Ltd.   Denver, Tokyo and Hong Kong

Publisher:
ARC International Ltd.

Corporate Headquarters
5445 DTC Parkway, Suite 720
Englewood, CO 80111 USA

Asian Headquarters
No. 32 Kowa Building 7th Floor
5-2-32 Minami Azabu
Minato-ku, Tokyo 106, Japan

Library of Congress Cataloging in Publication Data

Lynn, Dianna, 1955–
    One world, one child : expressions of childhood / by Dianna Lynn :
photographs by Yoshiaki Nagashima with lyrics by Joe Henry.
        p.   cn.
    ISBN: 4-900422-03-7
    1. Children—Pictorial works.   I. Nagashima, Yoshiaki, 1941–   .
II. Henry, Joe, 1943–   .   III. Title.
HQ781.5.L96 1991
305.23'022'2—dc20   91–27810
                               CIP

Printed in Japan.

NEPAL.

W̶e dedicate this book to all the children of the world. All profits from the sale of *One World, One Child* will provide support to nonprofit organizations committed to enhancing the quality of children's lives.

6 ONE WORLD ONE CHILD

PREFACE

I first met Levi while he was visiting his aunt, a close friend of mine. As our children played with a new puppy, their delightful laughter failed to mask the silence of the small boy who hid in the corner. He obviously lacked the spontaneity, curiosity and simple joy of other three-year olds. Drug addiction had not only poisoned his mother's life, but his as well. It was clear that he needed help. Later, my husband, Robert White, and I discussed whether or not there was something positive we could do to alter the course of Levi's life. Considering our options at length, we decided to bring him into our family. We felt he needed committed, loving parents and a stable environment where he could develop and grow.

I was well-meaning but naive. I saw myself as a rescuer who would bring miracles into Levi's life by giving him a nurturing home. We soon learned that we had embarked on a frequently horrifying journey that allowed no turning back. Step by step, we discovered the depth of the neglect and abuse, even torture, that Levi had suffered. The early years of his life, which should have secured for him an unqualified source of love—his bonding-time with his mother—had been shattered by abuse and abandonment.

Levi's days with us were a continuous flood of uncontrolled emotion. His early childhood experiences translated into trauma for all of us. During the two and a half years that he lived with us, we exhausted every imaginable method of reaching him. It was only after he inflicted severe burns on his younger sister's hand and later dislocated his infant sister's shoulder, that we acknowledged he needed help beyond our experience.

Levi now resides in a twenty-four hour therapeutic

BHUTAN

home with clinically-trained foster parents. His special environment is designed to assist him in healing his past and to teach him that by learning to love himself, he can learn to love others. By releasing his own pain, he can understand the pain he inflicted on others. And, by learning to make constructive choices, he will hopefully choose to create a promising future. We continue to love him. Our hope is that one day he will rejoin our family and share with us his special gifts.

I have spent many hours in therapy with Levi. As he has accessed his pain, the little girl in me has accessed hers. As he expressed his anger at being abused and abandoned, the little girl in me expressed hers as well. The human tragedy represented by Levi's early years and his healing process encouraged me to seek my own healing, to recover my own childlike faith, and to regain self-acceptance and self-love.

My wish for Levi, myself, and the child in us all, is that the promise of childhood be regained and that we give expression to the wonder and magic that live in our hearts.

One World, One Child was inspired by, and is dedicated to, that wish.

—DIANNA LYNN

INTRODUCTION

HONG KONG

NO TREASURE SURPASSES CHILDREN states an old Japanese proverb. Life's most consequential act is when we choose to create the opportunity for another human being to come forth, to draw breath, and to taste the sweetness of life. That the life we help create is also heir to all of humanity's sorrow is of no less import. It is for each of us to make the child's journey more providential, more welcome, and to fill the child's eyes with a true joy for being alive. We must honor and nurture the unique gifts that are inherent in each new life. These gifts sustain the magic of childhood and, in so doing, illuminate the rich mosaic of humanity.

The essential experiences of childhood are the same, no matter where they occur. The child I was, the experiences I had that tempered me, are with me today. Most memories I celebrate and cherish; some are hidden as far from my waking self as possible; others verge on the brink of expression awaiting their chance to live again. Though my body and mind have grown, the wisdom and wonder of the child still lives within me. It grounds and renews me. I have only to listen.

The photographs in *One World, One Child* express the magic of childhood. Presented here are children of all ages being with friends and family in near and distant lands. I have not met these children, yet I exist in each photograph. I share each child's dreams, challenges and promise. When we are in touch with the child-place within us and value ourselves and others, we create the opportunity to transform our future. Like placing crayon on blank paper, there is no limit to what can be designed. With each unique mark we make, and the intertwining of our differences, we create the human legacy. Thus we can create a more regenerative and sustainable environment for ourselves, our children and our planet. Children are our most precious natural resource. *No treasure surpasses children.*

As we celebrate the dynamic power of childhood, we find the spark that fuels our own inner child and once again look upon the world with wonder and renewed hope and faith. From that special place within me, I invite you to journey through *One World, One Child* and celebrate yourself in these children.

Our children are the possibility . . .

"Like a bright star in heaven
That lights our way home
Like the flower that shattered the stone."

—DIANNA LYNN

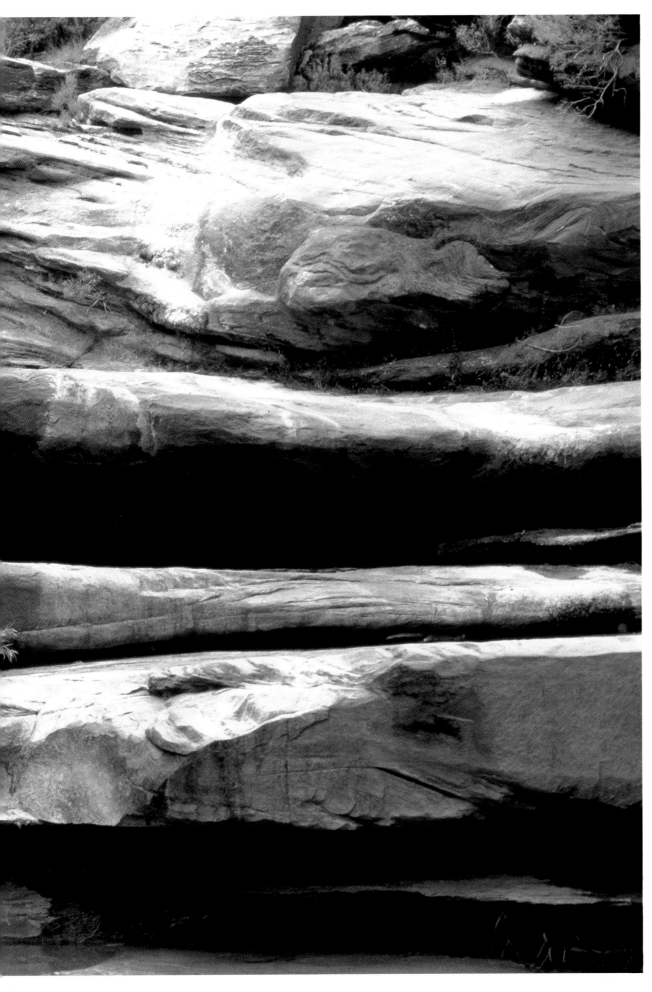

THE FLOWER THAT SHATTERED THE STONE

Earth is our mother

Just turning around

With her trees in the forest

And roots underground

Our father above us

Whose sigh is the wind

Paint us a rainbow

Without any end

A sparrow finds freedom

Beholding the sun

In the infinite beauty

We're all joined in one

I reach out before me

And look to the sky

Did I hear someone whisper

Did something pass by

As the river runs freely

The mountain does rise

Let me touch with my fingers

And see with my eyes

In the hearts of the children

A pure love still grows

Like a bright star in heaven

That lights our way home

Like the flower that shattered the stone

INDIA

There are days to be crossed

As I search for the way

There are doors I must try

Though I might be afraid . . .

_____

from In My Time

LESOTHO

When my loneliness is all I have

That ties me to the ground

Being lost is just across

The bridge from being found

I close my eyes and listen to

The spring rain falling down

And the rain between my heartbeats

Makes a hungry eager sound

from Yes And Yes

GUATEMALA

Children know how to grow it seems

And morning light fills the night as they dream

Children's hands understand that soon

We all will rise like the flight of the moon

---

from Angels Asleep On The Wind

MEXICO

THAILAND

When the journey makes you weary

From all the pain you've seen

And shadow fills the valley

You recall as being green

Your heart can be your prison

But your heart can learn to fly

Just thank the fate that made your soul

From a hungry searching child

---

from From A Hungry Child

CANADA

CHINA

If what you see

Can speak to me

It's just because we're one

Within the whole

The common soul

The father and the son

from Wings

INDONESIA

Embrace the truth that fills your eyes

Behind the cloudy veil

Then let the vision lead you home

Like ships with eager sails

_____

from Seize The Day

I can't understand it

I won't even try

As deep as an ocean

That never runs dry

But I still believe it

I know that it's true

Everything is our teacher

Reaching me and you

———————————————

from Stony Walls

ECUADOR

INDONESIA

INDIA

USA

NEW ZEALAND

ECUADOR

There is no easy road to peace

For all the living here

But kindness and the basic good

Can grow up from our fears

Storm winds bend the strongest tree

But teach it how to dance

And every heart can use its pain

To learn to take another chance

---

from Beauty And The Beast

ONE WORLD ONE CHILD 33

IRELAND

If the kindness hidden in the heart

Can lift the cold and fill the dark

Why can't we be a little more

Than everything we've been before

Brotherhood's the last frontier

The trip is just to make it here

A dream that's light-years far away

And near as we are here today

from The Last Frontier

NEPAL

COOK ISLANDS

. . . but the dark is where

the light begins

_____

from Hold Me If You Can

HONG KONG

CHINA

We'll come together in a time

Beyond the reach of sorrow

Every creature touched with grace

And trusting in tomorrow . . .

To change the way we all have known

The road we're used to taking

The comet's tail, the wind-filled sail

The vision in the making

---

from Wings

I'll beckon you at sunrise

My children of the wing

Let sorrow blow right through you

Let joy be ours to bring

For home we all are going

Yes home we've always been

Around the hearth-fire dreaming

Of skies we'll fly again

---

from Dutch's Song

WESTERN SOMOA

AFGHANISTAN

Oh the wisdom is reaching

Far beyond what you see

True wisdom is seeking

All the best you can be

So delight in the journey

And the struggle it seems

While the spirit is learning

That we rise with our dreams

———————————————

from We Rise With Our Dreams

MOROCCO

LESOTHO

USA

To touch a child

Is a gentle thing

Like a falling leaf

Like a dreamer's wings

The world can't be

All the hate it seems

To touch a child

Is a loving thing

———————————

from To Touch A Child

YAP ISLANDS

Peaceful valleys, animals
And children asking me
Tell the story that you told
Of sailors drinking tea

Tell the one about the man
Who saddled up the wind
Pegasus and flying fish
And woodmen made of tin

———————————

from Pegasus

Children climbing on my arms

And pigeons on my head

Get thee up my little man

And dream a dream instead

Dream a dream of rocking-chairs

And flying through the night

Dream until the morning's come

And turned the dark to light

_____

from Pegasus

ARGHANISTAN

USA

A man can't recall

When he first learned to fall

Or the time when

He learned how to climb

But the dream is the thing

It's his anchor and wings

Both his soul and

The flame in his eyes

---

from We Rise With Our Dreams

CANADA

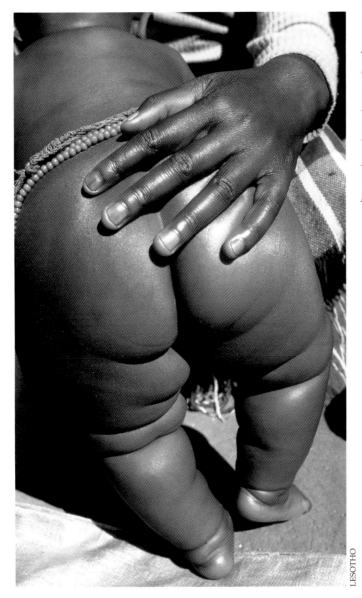

LESOTHO

We are still learning

Always returning

To one simple truth

Life is the proof

Love will provide

---

from Love Will Provide

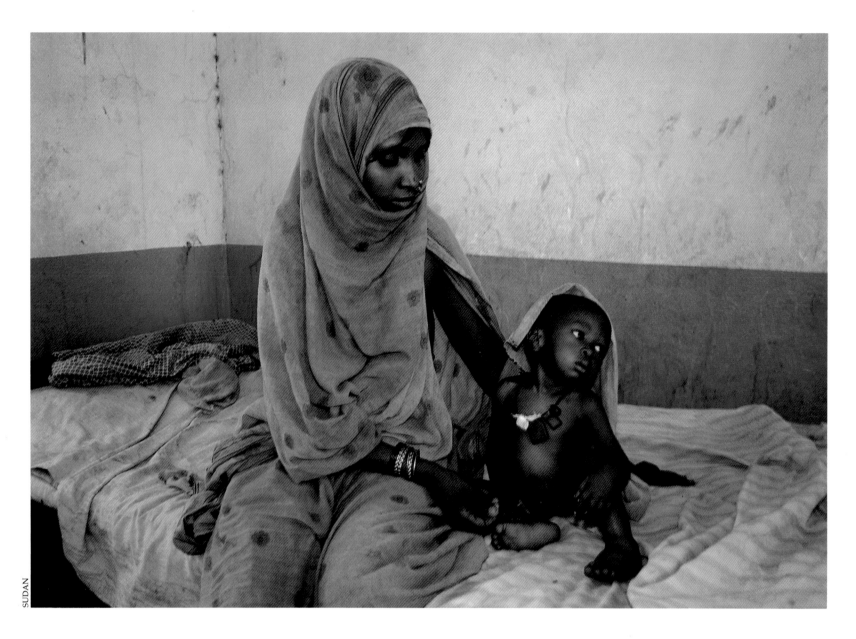

SUDAN

And every individual

Is every man you know

And every child in the dark

Deserves the right to grow

And every dream is holy

For the betterment of man

To strike the words 'it can't be done'

The children know it can

---

from Sticks & Stones

FRENCH POLYNESIA

INDONESIA

TIBET

There're windmills I must still ride down

And pinnacles to scale

Beaches I must rest upon

And oceans yet to sail

For lost horizons beckon me

And love I've never known

The dream beyond the reaching hand

The welcome lights of home

———————————————————

from Islands In The Stream

CHINA

ECUADOR

Weave yourself a tapestry
To keep your shoulders warm
Days well-spent in seeking out
The calm beyond the storm

Spend your days and harvest all
The good your soul can find
Then share the goodness of yourself
And drain the singing cup of time

from October/Tapestry

INDIA

We are children of the comet

We're all children of the sun

On a journey through the corridors of night

But you will grow to understand

And so you'll know the way

And you will be the rebirth of the light

---

from The Rebirth Of The Light

ST. LUCIA

Understand

If you can

Every heart

Plays its part

In the scheme

The common dream

The blessed mystery

_____

from Stony Walls

JAPAN

I've been accused of fearlessness

    By those who live in fear

A fallen angel torn between

    His hope and his despair

A frightened child who can't decide

    Just what he's come to find

A weary pilgrim with no thought

    Of what he's left behind

———————————————

from Seeker

So I'm searching for beginnings
As I try to understand
All the pathways that I've followed
Fading footprints in the sand

I'll pursue the far horizon
Reaching out with both my hands
Seeking out my own lone self
The child within the man

from The Child Within The Man

LESOTHO

PERU

In time is everything we need

In time we can forgive

In time our wounds become our strength

In time we'll learn to live

In time our love will be enough

In time we'll finally see

In time our vision will restore

The ancient harmony

from Beyond The Last Frontier

Gypsy ponies know the way

Their silver feet fly faster

Ah take me too to ride with you

With bells and children's laughter

———————————————

from The Man Who Runs The Carousel

USA

USSR

With each step that I take

I am nearer the end

Of the darkness that hides

All the light 'round the bend

---

from In My Time

Take a message to my daughter

And to my loving son

And tell the children of the world

Whose time is yet to come

Let them memorize a flower

Let them learn to love a song

Let them be too busy finding joy

To need to hide from right and wrong

Rainbow round

With children's hands

A bridge across the sky

Rainbow round

It's open hands

That let the children fly

---

from Let The Children Fly

NEPAL

JAPAN

FRANCE

The vision of your goodness

Will sustain me through the cold

Take my hand now to remember

When you find yourself alone

---

from The Wings That Fly Us Home

If wishes were eagles

And sparrows and doves

If wishes were warm lips

That whispered of love

If wishes were promises

Made on a star

Could we finish our wishing

And just be who we are

---

from Wishes

BRAZIL

And I hope that your hands grow

With the strength of your vision

And I hope in your dreaming you'll see

All your brothers and sisters

In a lovely earth garden

And that peace all together

is your sweet destiny

---

from The Rebirth Of The Light

FRANCE

The green things springing up from dust

Like songs upon the land

Our children laughing with delight

At seeds blown from their hands

The gentle creatures with their young

All scattered on the hills

The meaning of each moment

In the gift of life fulfilled

from Beyond The Last Frontier

MALDIVE ISLANDS

Solitary islands

Surrounded by the sea

Waiting for a foot to land

To free us from our dreams

We are what can be seen at once

And then we're something more

We are what lies so deep and dark

Behind the golden shore

———————————————

from Islands

THAILAND

BRAZIL

JAPAN

Oh come ye now unto the flame

Keep it through the night

Nourish it and share its warmth

And spend its precious light

The torch is passed among us all

To help us understand

A covenant of brotherhood

That joins our open hands

_____

from The Flame

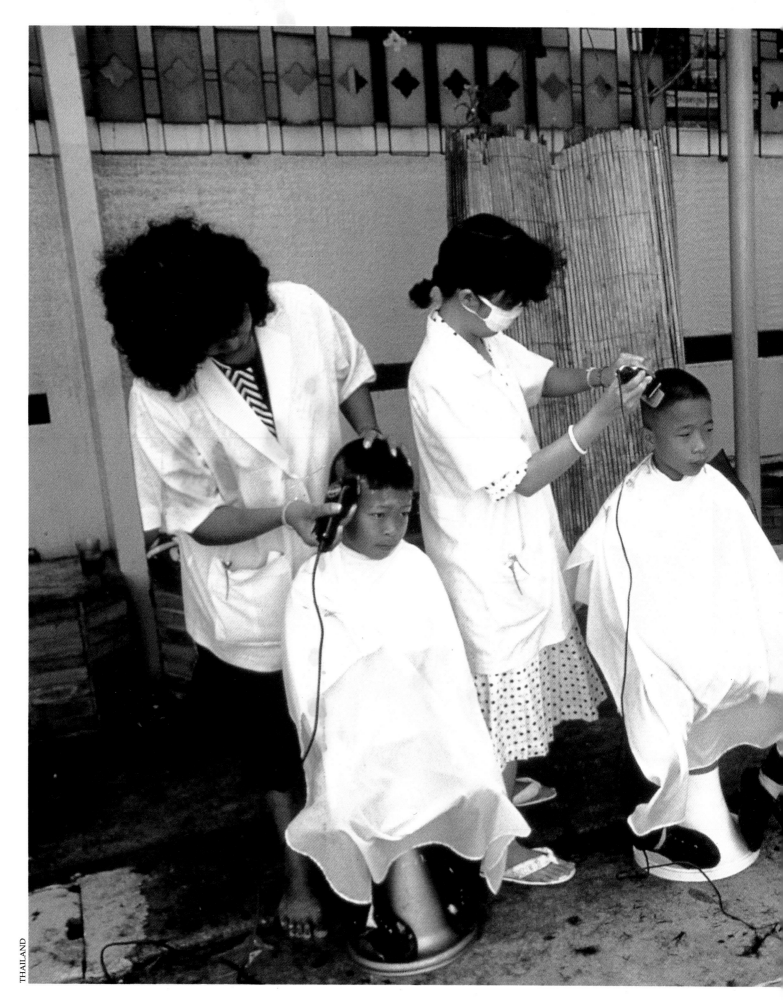

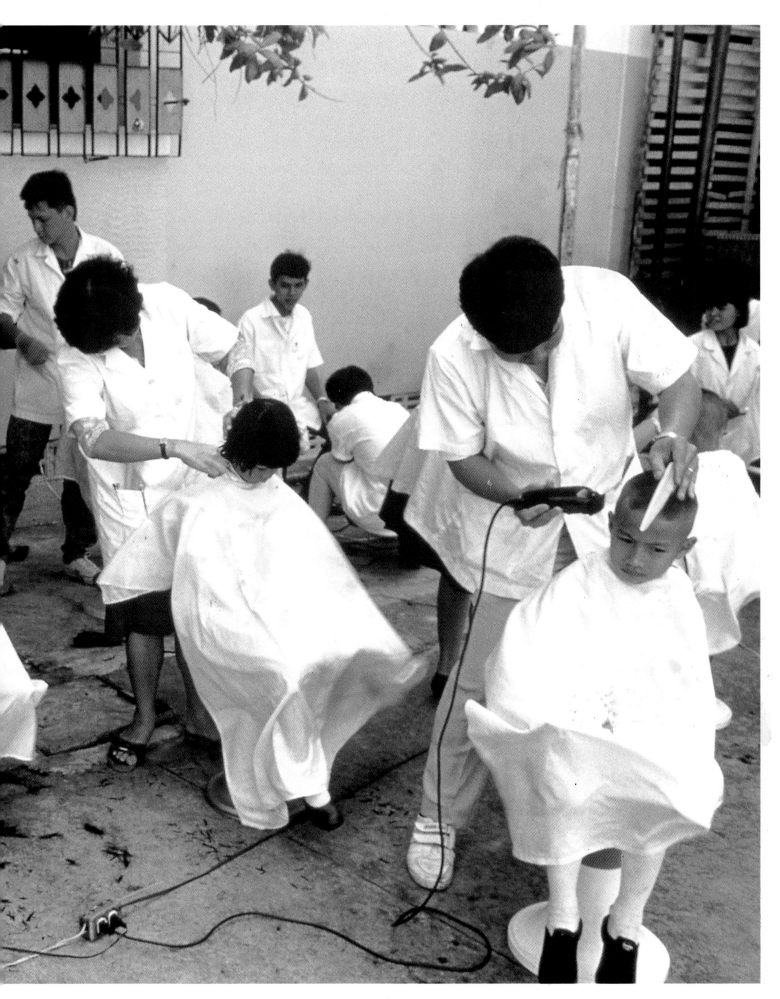

JAPAN

There're days to fall and days to rise

And days for making haste

Days for seeking out yourself

But no days you can waste . . .

———————————————

from Pegasus

We all can live together
We all can live in peace
We're all descended from one soul
One universal dream

To love the light while it is here
To comprehend the need
To cherish every breath of life
To nourish every seed

———————————————

from Have We Forgotten

FRANCE

THAILAND

Destiny will guide my hand
Until I learn to fly
And every new lesson that I learn
Still points me toward the sky

And obstacles that block the path
To wisdom's open door
Only make me know I will survive
I'll strive to be much more

---

from Dream High

So now I'm on my odyssey
I won't be back again
I pass this way one lonely time
I ride the cosmic wind

If you ever think to track me down
Just look up toward the sun
For a spirit on two golden wings
Whose journey's just begun

from New Worlds

AFGHANISTAN

We are all connected in the flow . . .

from Late For Changing

KENYA

EGYPT

NEPAL

ACKNOWLEDGMENTS

It is important to acknowledge that everyone who participated in the creation and production of *One World, One Child* did so from a personal commitment. Each is dedicated to the purpose of the book and made a personal difference by discounting or donating services. It is with heartfelt love and gratitude that I thank them individually and collectively.

In addition, I would like to thank my husband, Robert White, for his unending patience, encouragement and support in the process of healing my inner child and the expression of that healing through the creation of this book. I would like to acknowledge John Denver for his generosity, friendship and quiet support of who I am and the difference I strive to make in the world. Special thanks go to Carol Wingfield, for through her creativity, professionalism and willingness to do whatever was needed, the book became the best that it could be; to Janie Joseland Bennett, whose assistance in assembling the creative team can best be seen in the book's resulting beauty; to Joe Henry, who constantly challenged me to reach for the highest star and demand excellence of myself in pursuit of excellence for *One World, One Child*.

Thanks to Riva Greenberg, Tamiko Kawashima, Yuko Sugahara and the fine team of translators and editors they assembled to create the Japanese edition. Thanks to John Babbs, Ellie Fox, Jan Fox, Caren Head, Anna Huff, Diana Leigh, Sandie Madison, Monica McGrath, Patricia Neeb, Shelley Saban, Stephanie Sherman and all my family and friends whose love and support have brought life to this dream long held in my heart.

A special acknowledgment to Yoshiaki Nagashima, Photographers/Aspen and the following music publishers: Cool Hand Music, Tree Publishing, Inspector Barlow Music and Cherry Lane Music, whose commitment to enhancing the quality of children's lives is demonstrated by their contribution to *One World, One Child*.

To John, Lynn, Jim, Michael, Connell and Foster, whose love and commitment to Levi's well being is an inspiration. Your work to heal the heart lights our way home. I am deeply grateful. —DIANNA LYNN

THE AUTHOR

Dianna Lynn, executive vice-president of ARC International, is known for her expertise in human resource management and communication skills training. Transferring her business acumen to philanthropic activities, she participated in fundraising efforts for the Special Olympics in the Pacific Northwest, the Rocky Mountain Adoption Exchange, and the Karitas and Kempe Children's Foundations. While living in Tokyo for four years and traveling to refugee villages and

ECUADOR

orphanages in Sri Lanka, she began to focus her attention on global children's issues. She continues to work with the Sri Lanka Sarvodaya Community Development Organization and the One World One People Foundation in conjunction with ARC International. She draws upon her varied experiences of rearing six children, the unique memories of her own childhood and her many friendships with children from around the world to create *One World, One Child*.

THE PHOTOGRAPHERS

Yoshiaki Nagashima travels the world as he lives out a twenty-year commitment to capture every nation's people on film. His organization, The Brain Center, is headquartered in Osaka, Japan. A graduate of the Nihon Professional School of Photography, he is a member of the Japan Photographers' Association. His work has been widely exhibited in Japan and China, and is available in a number of multi-lingual books, including *One World, One People* and *A Day in the Life of Japan*. He has also produced a popular Senshukai travel series, Bunkasha's world culture series, and a volume on the castles of Europe.

Photographers/Aspen, a consortium of freelance photographers, contributed selected images to complement those of Nagashima. For over two decades, their distinctive photographs have depicted the world as it is: forgotten, hidden, revealed and rediscovered. **Nicholas DeVore III**, through extensive study and travel, has recorded sensitive and exotic images that have appeared in *National Geographic*, and such works as *A Day in the Life of Japan* and *Seven Days in the Kingdom of Thailand*. He has taught at workshops throughout the U.S. and is a frequent lecturer for the Explorer's Club. **Paul Chesley**, a freelance photographer with the National Geographic Society since 1975, has been featured internationally in museums and in such publications as *Life*, *Fortune*, *Geo* and *Travel & Leisure*. He has participated in eleven *Day in the Life* projects, and recently photographed Australian Aborigines for *The Circle of Life*. **David Hiser**'s adventure-oriented style combines photographic and outdoor skills to capture subjects ranging from remote cultures to urban projects. He has recently completed his 55th assignment for *National Geographic*. **Chris Rainier**, also a *National Geographic* contributor, was inspired by his four years as assistant to photographer Ansel Adams, and has documented more than 33 countries' landscapes and cultures. His long term projects include photographing refugee camps and sacred places around the globe. **Melinda Berge** is an award-winning and internationally published photographer whose works have appeared in *National Geographic*, *Smithsonian* and *Paris Match*.

THE LYRICIST

Joe Henry has written lyrics to more than fifty recordings, performed by such varied artists as Frank Sinatra, John Denver, Roberta Flack, Olivia Newton-John, and Kenny Rogers. His acclaimed stage-presentation, *Prelude to Lime Creek*, with renowned actor Anthony Zerbe and popular recording-artists John Jarvis and Michael Johnson, was devised from his novel-in-progress, "Lime Creek." His primary musical collaborators have been John Denver and John Jarvis, while his poetry and prose have been interpreted theatrically by Anthony Zerbe and Roscoe Lee Browne.

PRODUCTION NOTES

The design of *One World, One Child* was developed and coordinated by **Carol Wingfield**, founder and creative director of BodyCopy, Inc. (Washington, DC). During her eleven years as art director for Heldref Publications, she was responsible for the design and production of over 40 educational journals and magazines. **Robert Maraziti** of Snowmass, Colorado made additional design contributions to this book.

The photo editor is **Janie Joseland Bennett**, director of Photographers/Aspen (Aspen, Colorado). She has recently participated in such book projects as *Malaysia: Cultural Heart of South East Asia* and *The Circle of Life*. Editorial direction was provided by **Joe Henry** with technical support from **Nancy Roach** of the Aspen School District and **Christina Young** of New York City.

Printing consulting services were provided by **Stephanie Sherman** of San Francisco, California.

The English edition of this book was produced in a Macintosh-based computer environment by BodyCopy, Inc. (Washington, DC) with digital imaging services provided by PS Computer Graphics and linotronic output by Travis Halperin/IzzaGraphics of Boulder and Aspen, Colorado respectively. Production for the Japanese edition was coordinated by **Riva Greenberg**, **Kiyoshi Tabata** and their assistant, **Tomoko Kitajima** of ARC International Ltd. (Tokyo). The supervisors of the translation team were **Tamiko Kawashima** and **Yuko Sugahara**. Typesetting and design services were provided by **Koichi Hama**.

Color separations, printing and bindery services were provided by Dai Nippon Printing Company, Ltd. (Tokyo, Japan) and coordinated by **Noboru Watanabe** of DNP America, Inc. (San Francisco, California).

Special thanks are extended to Jessica Mezyk and Chuck Savitt for their encouragement and support of the production effort.

CREDITS

PHOTOGRAPHS (*Page numbers are indicated in* **bold.**): **Front cover**, Yoshiaki Nagashima; **1**, Nicholas DeVore III/Photographers Aspen; **2**, Yoshiaki Nagashima; **5**, Yoshiaki Nagashima; **6**, Paul Chesley/Photographers Aspen; **7**, Paul Chesley/Photographers Aspen; **8**, Yoshiaki Nagashima; **9**, Yoshiaki Nagashima; **10/11**, Nicholas DeVore III/Photographers Aspen; **12**, Yoshiaki Nagashima; **13**, Yoshiaki Nagashima; **14**, Nicholas DeVore III/Photographers Aspen; **15**, David Hiser/Photographers Aspen; **16**, David Hiser/Photographers Aspen; 17, Nicholas DeVore III/Photographers Aspen; **18**, Paul Chesley/Photographers Aspen; **19**, Paul Chesley/Photographers Aspen; **20/21**, Yoshiaki Nagashima; **22**, David Hiser/Photographers Aspen; **23**, Yoshiaki Nagashima; **24**, Nicholas DeVore III/Photographers Aspen; **25**, Yoshiaki Nagashima; **26**, Paul Chesley/Photographers Aspen; **27**, Melinda Berge/Photographers Aspen; **28**, Paul Chesley/Photographers Aspen; **29**, Nicholas DeVore III/Photographers Aspen; **30**, Nicholas DeVore III/Photographers Aspen; **31**, Paul Chesley/Photographers Aspen; **32**, Nicholas DeVore III/Photographers Aspen; **33**, Nicholas DeVore III/Photographers Aspen; **34**, Nicholas DeVore III/Photographers Aspen; **35**, Nicholas DeVore III/Photographers Aspen; **36/37**, Nicholas DeVore III/Photographers Aspen; **38**, Nicholas DeVore III/Photographers Aspen; **39**, Yoshiaki Nagashima; **40**, Yoshiaki Nagashima; **41**, Nicholas DeVore III/Photographers Aspen; **42/43**, Yoshiaki Nagashima; **44**, David Hiser/Photographers Aspen; **45**, Yoshiaki Nagashima; **46**, Yoshiaki Nagashima; **47**, Nicholas DeVore III/Photographers Aspen; **48**, Yoshiaki Nagashima; **49**, Nicholas DeVore III/Photographers Aspen; **50**, Nicholas DeVore III/Photographers Aspen; **51**, David Hiser/Photographers Aspen; **52/53**, Yoshiaki Nagashima; **54**, David Hiser/Photographers Aspen; **55**, David Hiser/Photographers Aspen; **56/57**, Paul Chesley/Photographers Aspen; **58**, Yoshiaki Nagashima; **59**, Nicholas DeVore III/Photographers Aspen; **60/61**, Paul Chesley/Photographers Aspen; **62**, Chris Rainier/Photographers Aspen; **63**, Nicholas DeVore III/Photographers Aspen; **64**, Yoshiaki Nagashima; **65**, Yoshiaki Nagashima; **66**, Yoshiaki Nagashima; **67**, Paul Chesley/Photographers Aspen; **68**, Paul Chesley/Photographers Aspen; **69**, Yoshiaki Nagashima; **70/71**, Nicholas DeVore III/Photographers Aspen; **72**, Yoshiaki Nagashima; **73**, Paul Chesley/Photographers Aspen; **74**, Paul Chesley/Photographers Aspen; **75**, Yoshiaki Nagashima; **76/77**, Paul Chesley/Photographers Aspen; **78**, Nicholas DeVore III/Photographers Aspen; **79**, Nicholas DeVore III/Photographers Aspen; **80**, Nicholas DeVore III/Photographers Aspen; **81**, Paul Chesley/Photographers Aspen; **82/83**, Nicholas DeVore III/Photographers Aspen; **84**, Yoshiaki Nagashima; **85**, Yoshiaki Nagashima; **86**, Paul Chesley/Photographers Aspen; **87**, Yoshiaki Nagashima; **88/89**, Paul Chesley/Photographers Aspen; **90**, Nicholas DeVore III/Photographers Aspen; **91**, Yoshiaki Nagashima; **92/93**, Nicholas DeVore III/Photographers Aspen; **94**, Yoshiaki Nagashima; **95**, Yoshiaki Nagashima; **96**, Paul Chesley/Photographers Aspen; **97**, Nicholas DeVore III/Photographers Aspen; **98**, Yoshiaki Nagashima; **99**, Yoshiaki Nagashima; **100/101**, Paul Chesley/Photographers Aspen; **102**, Paul Chesley/Photographers Aspen; **103**, Yoshiaki Nagashima; **104/105**, Yoshiaki Nagashima; **106**, Yoshiaki Nagashima; **107**, Yoshiaki Nagashima; **108**, Yoshiaki Nagashima; **109**, Paul Chesley/Photographers Aspen; **110/111**, Yoshiaki Nagashima; **112**, David Hiser/Photographers Aspen; **113**, Yoshiaki Nagashima; **114**, Yoshiaki Nagashima; **115**, Yoshiaki Nagashima; **116**, Yoshiaki Nagashima; **117**, Nicholas DeVore III/Photographers Aspen; **118**, Paul Chesley/Photographers Aspen; **Back cover**, Yoshiaki Nagashima.

LYRICS (*Used by permission. All rights reserved. Page numbers are indicated in* **bold.**): **Pages 9 and 11**, *The Flower That Shattered The Stone*. Copyright 1988 by Cool Hand Music/Tree Publishing. Lyrics by Joe Henry/music by John Jarvis. **13**, from *In My Time*. Copyright 1990 by Cool Hand Music/Inspector Barlow Music. Lyrics by Joe Henry/music by John Jarvis. **15**, from *Yes And Yes*. Copyright 1985 by Joe Henry. Lyrics by Joe Henry/music by John Jarvis. **16**, from *Angels Asleep On The Wind*. Copyright 1987 by Joe Henry. **21**, from *From A Hungry Child*. Copyright 1973 by Joe Henry. **23**, from *Wings*. Copyright 1979 by Joe Henry. Lyrics by Joe Henry/music by John Jarvis. **24**, from *Seize The Day*. Copyright 1984 by Joe Henry. **25**, from *Stony Walls*. Copyright 1990 by Joe Henry. **32**, from *Beauty And The Beast*. Copyright 1988 by Joe Henry. **34**, from *The Last Frontier*. Copyright 1983 by Joe Henry. **39**, from *Hold Me If You Can*. Copyright 1973 by Joe Henry. **41**, from *Wings*. Copyright 1979 by Joe Henry. Lyrics by Joe Henry/music by John Jarvis. **43**, from *Dutch's Song*. Copyright 1982 by Joe Henry. **45**, from *We Rise With Our Dreams*. Copyright 1987 by Cool Hand Music/Tree Publishing. Lyrics by Joe Henry/music by John Jarvis. **50**, from *To Touch A Child*. Copyright 1970 by Joe Henry. Lyrics by Joe Henry/music by Tom Bähler. **51**, from *Pegasus*. Copyright 1974 by Cherry Lane Music. Lyrics by Joe Henry/music by John Denver. **52**, from *Pegasus*. Copyright 1974 by Cherry Lane Music. Lyrics by Joe Henry/music by John Denver. **54**, from *We Rise With Our Dreams*. Copyright 1987 by Cool Hand Music/Tree Publishing. Lyrics by Joe Henry/music by John Jarvis. **59**, from *Love Will Provide*. Copyright 1989 by Cool Hand Music/Tree Publishing. Lyrics by Joe Henry/music by John Jarvis. **62**, from *Sticks & Stones*. Copyright 1977 by Joe Henry. **66**, from *Islands In The Stream*. Copyright 1978 by Joe Henry. **68**, from *October/Tapestry*. Copyright 1974 by Joe Henry. **71**, from *The Rebirth Of The Light*. Copyright 1986 by Joe Henry. **72**, from *Stony Walls*. Copyright 1990 by Joe Henry. **75**, from *Seeker*. Copyright 1978 by Joe Henry. **77**, from *The Child Within The Man*. Copyright 1969 by Joe Henry. Lyrics by Joe Henry/music by Bobby Scott. **79**, from *Beyond The Last Frontier*. Copyright 1977 by Joe Henry. **80**, from *The Man Who Runs The Carousel*. Copyright 1969 by Joe Henry. **81**, from *In My Time*. Copyright 1990 by Cool Hand Music/Inspector Barlow Music. Lyrics by Joe Henry/music by John Jarvis. **82**, from *Let The Children Fly*. Copyright 1980 by Cool Hand Music/Cherry Lane Music. Lyrics by Joe Henry/music by Lee Holdridge. **87**, from *The Wings That Fly Us Home*. Copyright 1976 by Cherry Lane Music. Lyrics by Joe Henry/music by John Denver. **89**, from *Wishes*. Copyright 1981 by Joe Henry. Lyrics by Joe Henry/music by Donna Fargo. **91**, from *The Rebirth Of The Light*. Copyright 1986 by Joe Henry. **93**, from *Beyond The Last Frontier*. Copyright 1977 by Joe Henry. **94**, from *Islands*. Copyright 1981 by Joe Henry. Lyrics by Joe Henry/music by John Jarvis. **98**, from *The Flame*, copyright 1990 by Joe Henry. Lyrics by Joe Henry/music by John Jarvis. **103**, from *Pegasus*. Copyright 1974 by Cherry Lane Music. Lyrics by Joe Henry/music by John Denver. **105**, from *Have We Forgotten*. Copyright 1985 by Joe Henry. **110**, from *Dream High*. Copyright 1989 by Joe Henry. **112**, from *New Worlds*. Copyright 1973 by Joe Henry. **113**, from *Late For Changing*. Copyright 1988 by Cool Hand Music/Tree Publishing. Lyrics by Joe Henry/music by John Jarvis.